FEELINGS

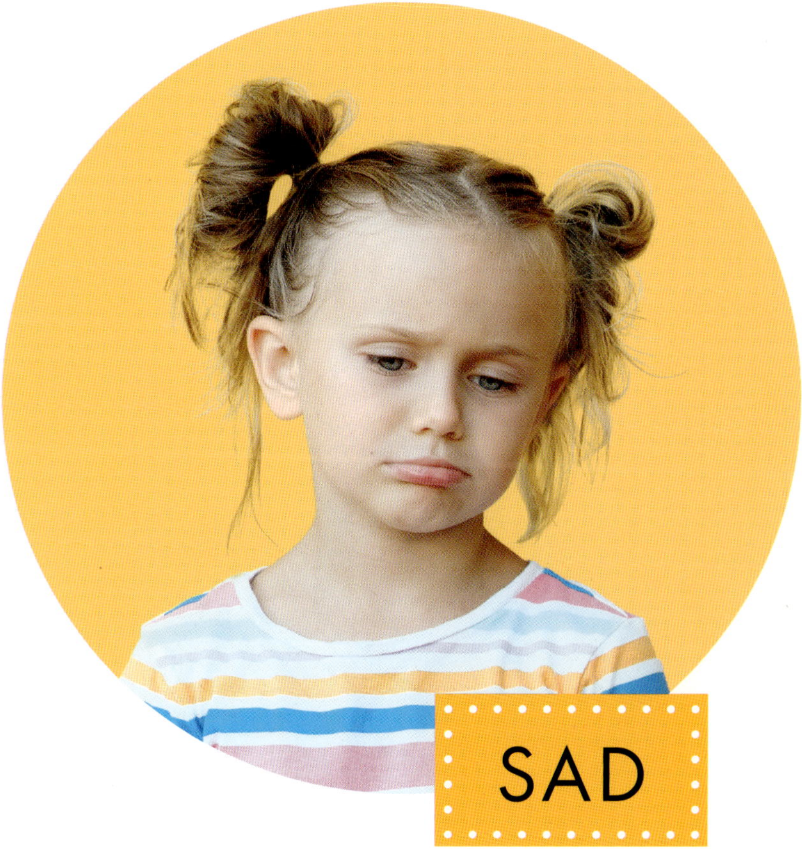

SAD

by Alissa Thielges

crying

frown

Look for these words and pictures as you read.

head down

hug

Sadness is a feeling.
It means you feel down.

Sam feels sad.
His toy broke.
He frowns.

head down

Dan's feelings are hurt.
His friends play without him.
His chest feels tight.
His head hangs down.

Bree feels unhappy.
She can't go to the park.
She asks for a hug.

hug

crying

Mary is very sad.
Her dog died.
She is crying.

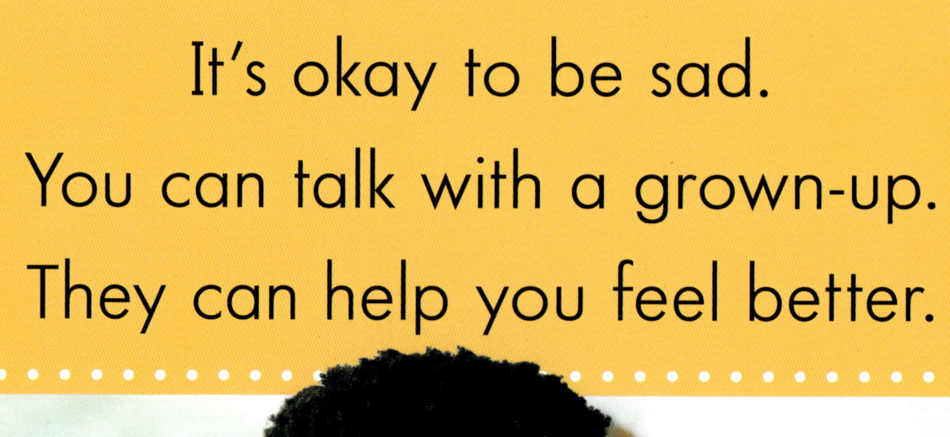
It's okay to be sad.
You can talk with a grown-up.
They can help you feel better.

People are sad for different reasons.
What makes you sad?

crying

frown

Did you find?

head down

hug

Spot is published by Amicus Learning, an imprint of Amicus
P.O. Box 227, Mankato, MN 56002
www.amicuspublishing.us

Library of Congress Cataloging-in-Publication Data
Names: Thielges, Alissa, 1995– author.
Title: Sad / by Alissa Thielges.
Description: Mankato, MN : Amicus Learning, [2025] |
    Series: Spot feelings | Audience: Ages 4–7 | Audience:
    Grades K–1 | Summary: "What makes kids feel sad?
    Encourage social-emotional learning with this beginning
    reader that introduces vocabulary for discussing feelings
    of sadness with an engaging search-and-find feature"—
    Provided by publisher.
Identifiers: LCCN 2024017563 (print) | LCCN 2024017564
    (ebook) | ISBN 9798892000826 (library binding) |
    ISBN 9798892001403 (paperback) |
    ISBN 9798892001984 (ebook)
Subjects: LCSH: Sadness in children—Juvenile literature. |
    Sadness—Juvenile literature.
Classification: LCC BF723.S15 T54 2025 (print) | LCC
    BF723.S15 (ebook) | DDC 152.4—dc23/eng/20240502
LC record available at https://lccn.loc.gov/2024017563
LC ebook record available at https://lccn.loc.
    gov/2024017564

Printed in China

Ana Brauer, editor
Deb Miner, series designer
Kim Pfeffer, book designer
and photo researcher

Photos by Adobe Stock/polya_olya,
cover; Alamy Stock Photo/Leonid
Iastremskyi, 3; Freepik/leberus777, 14,
mawats, 1, nimito, 6–7, Wavebreak
Media, 12–13; Shutterstock/AAAstudios,
10–11, esthermm, 4–5, Tijana Moraca, 8